WHO MARCHED FOR CIVIL RIGHTS?

Richard Spilsbury

raintree

a Capstone company — publishers for children

WHAT WERE CIVIL RIGHTS?

Little Rock was separated ... there were the white ladies bathroom and the black ladies bathroom... one day, I ... decided that I wanted to know what was in a white ladies bathroom that I couldn't see ... so I went in there and, here are all these cops banging on the door ... my mother was screaming "Don't kill her!"... And there was nothing but toilets in there.

Melba Pattillo

Melba Pattillo was a teenager in the town of Little Rock, Arkansas, in the 1950s. The quote above is from an interview in later life describing what she experienced as a girl. Melba was just one of millions of US citizens who couldn't choose where to go to the toilet, eat, study, or sit on a bus because she was black.

The **US Constitution** said all Americans were equal citizens. But a famous court case called Plessy v. Ferguson in 1896 established the idea that states could insist on "separate but equal" treatment for citizens based on their skin colour or race. Most black people in the US lived in states such as Arkansas in **the South**. Following the court case, every southern state had created **Jim Crow laws**. These made it law for black citizens to have separate, poorer public facilities and work opportunities, and fewer chances to improve their status than white people. This was racial **segregation**.

CIVIL RIGHTS MOVEMENT

Most people believe that everyone should have the right to say what they think, vote for the leaders they want, receive equal protection from the law, and not face **discrimination**. These are civil rights. There have been struggles in many countries to improve the civil rights of different groups of people, but the **civil rights movement** usually refers to the decade or so from the mid-1950s when black Americans struggled to gain key civil rights.

This was a difficult and often violent struggle for the people involved. Here is what happened when Melba Pattillo tried to enrol at the whites-only Central High School in Little Rock:

> … there [was] a mob in front of the school … filled with layers …
> of red-faced angry people … jeering… [Then] I saw all these
> faces looking at me … what they're turning around for is to kill you…
> I back up in astonishment … and my mother just screamed at me,
> she said, "I tell you, get to the car now! Listen to me, leave me if
> you have to, get to the car!" … we both got in the car… and we
> [escaped from the] mob.

Education, public accommodation, and transport

Transport

Education

Education and transport

▲ From the late 19th century to the mid-20th century, Jim Crow laws of various sorts were official in most southern and eastern states of the United States. This map shows what categories of Jim Crow laws applied in each state.

GRADUAL CHANGE

In the 1950s, there was growing frustration amongst black Americans about segregation. Some had recently returned home from World War II, where they had fought in the same forces as white soldiers against the same enemies. Many felt that Nazi **persecution** and segregation of Jewish people was similar to the treatment of black people in the United States. In some states, Jim Crow laws were gradually changing. This was partly through the increasing role of the **National Association for the Advancement of Colored People (NAACP)**. The group's founders included W.E.B. DuBois, the first black person to gain a doctorate from Harvard University, and Mary White Ovington, a white woman whose grandparents had worked to end slavery in the 19th century. NAACP members gave financial and legal support to help black people fight court cases to, for example, gain equal educational opportunities.

DOLL TEST

Psychologists Kenneth and Mamie Clark presented the results of their Doll test as evidence at Brown v. Board of Education. Black children were shown four plastic dolls, identical except for the colour of their "skin". They said they preferred to play with the white doll and attributed more positive characteristics to it than the black one. Doctors concluded that "prejudice, discrimination, and segregation" caused black children to develop a sense of inferiority and self-hatred.

▼ NAACP lawyer Thurgood Marshall (see page 9) speaking to reporters.

BROWN V. BOARD OF EDUCATION

In 1954, the lead NAACP lawyer Thurgood Marshall and his team won a very important legal case called **Brown v. Board of Education**. They presented evidence to the **US Supreme Court** from five state court cases in which black people had been unsuccessful at ending school segregation. This included photos of poor conditions in black schools and psychologists' reports proving how segregation harmed black children.

The Supreme Court concluded that all segregation of public schools was illegal. This was a significant step in improving civil rights for black Americans, but there was great resistance to changing Jim Crow school segregation laws in the South. A student named James A. Banks recalls that: "The white school boards controlled both black and white schools. Consequently, for black teachers to spread the word about the [Brown v. Board] decision, especially among students, would probably have been considered a subversive and dangerous act."

HISTORY DETECTIVES: WHAT IS RESEARCH?

Historical research starts with one or more questions or problems we want to resolve. Research can be very time-consuming, so how do you start and keep on track?

One way is by using a KWL chart. This is a graphic organizer with three columns headed "what I know", "what I want to know", and "what I have learned". The first column is your chance to say what you already know or think you know about the topic. Use the second column to help you focus on what is required in your research. Your research results can go in the last column.

TAKING ACTION

Most schools in the South remained segregated after Brown v. Board of Education because forcing change through legal cases was slow. From the mid-1950s onwards, more and more civil rights protestors took **direct action** to try to speed up change. Direct action is when people carry out public acts that disrupt or break the law in order to raise awareness of an issue. Rosa Parks refusing to give up her seat to a white woman on a public bus in Montgomery, Alabama, in 1955 was an early example. The NAACP planned this action, and used Rosa's arrest to spark a **boycott** of city buses. After 13 months of lost business and bad publicity, the state made segregation illegal on its buses.

Other famous examples of taking action for civil rights in the 1950s include the Little Rock Nine. Nine black children, including Melba Pattillo, tried to attend a white-only school in 1957. The resulting violence and protests from people against segregation led to the US government stepping in to force the governor of Arkansas, Orval Faubus, to **desegregate** its schools. Watch an interview with Governor Faubus in which he explains why he prevented the Little Rock Nine going to school: www.hrc.utexas.edu/multimedia/video/2008/wallace/faubus_orval.html.

▼ Fifteen-year-old Elizabeth Eckford (in sunglasses) walks past angry white students during the Little Rock Nine action.

ORVAL FAUBUS
1910–1994

BORN: Combs, Arkansas

ROLE: Governor of Arkansas from 1954 to 1967. In 1957, he ordered the **National Guard** to stop black children going to Little Rock High School to keep law and order. US President Dwight D. Eisenhower ordered government troops in to protect the Little Rock Nine so they could attend school.

Did You Know?

Faubus ended segregation in Arkansas on state public transport when he was first elected governor.

DANGER

It is difficult to imagine now how strongly some white people felt about civil rights campaigners in the 1950s. Many were members of groups such as the Ku Klux Klan (KKK). The KKK was a terrorist organization whose actions included **firebombing** homes and churches, and **lynching**. Lynching involved a mob seizing, beating, and usually violently killing people. In 1957, for example, the KKK offered a $10,000 reward to anyone who killed one of the Little Rock Nine.

HISTORY DETECTIVES: SOURCES

Diaries, interviews, autobiographies, and photos are primary sources, or records of events created at the time under study. Secondary sources are interpretations and analyses of primary sources. They are usually created by people who weren't there at the time. Examples include books, biographies, and films. Secondary sources can provide good overviews to direct research, but a range of primary sources can add details and bring the past to life.

WHY DID PEOPLE MARCH FOR CIVIL RIGHTS?

From winter 1961, civil rights protestors in Albany, Georgia, ran a campaign to end segregation on buses. Hundreds of volunteers (many of whom were students) met in churches. They marched to and occupied the bus station. They recited prayers and sang songs together, refusing to be moved on by police. One protestor, Bernice Johnson Reagon, recalls how it felt:

> For many people like me, the highest point of our lives was when we gathered in those mass meetings, and when we marched ... we were bonded to each other, not because we went to school together, or were in the same social club. Not because we worked on the same job, but because we had decided that we would put everything on the line to fight racism in our community.

▼ These Albany marchers kneel and pray before being arrested for marching in 1961.

Protestors expected a violent response from Albany police, but instead they were peacefully arrested. The campaign – called the Albany Movement – continued for many months. More than 1,000 people were arrested and taken to prisons outside the county to prevent further protests around Albany's prisons. Many people describe Albany as a failure in the civil rights movement because it did not end with desegregation and organizers had to spend a lot of money getting protestors out of prison. Yet this was the first time that a large civil rights march had taken place, and it made it clear to organizers that mass protests could have a big impact.

HISTORY DETECTIVES: A BALANCED VIEW

Primary sources about the same events can express very different opinions. In the examples below, two newspaper editorials describe the same march in Albany. However, one reports that it was a nuisance for the locals and the other says it was a nuisance that the civil rights movement had to go through another unnecessary struggle. In your research, it is very useful to show both sides because it can highlight different feelings about the same moments in history.

Editorial:
Albany Bears Up Well
Our sympathy goes out to the people of Albany, over their difficulty. The patient restraint they have exhibited, the good judgment shown by their officials and especially the manner in which Albany's chief of police has enforced the law and maintained order has won the admiration of countless thousands.
The Birmingham Post-Herald
4 August 1962

Editorial:
Another Round in a Wasteful Fight
The latest racial incident in Albany, Georgia, is depressing, not because of violence, for there was none, but because it is but another dreary round in a fight so wasteful of human energy. The eventual outcome of the struggle is no longer in doubt. Segregation is doomed, and even the extreme **segregationists** know they are only engaged in a holding action...
The Louisville Courier Journal
16 July 1962

MARCHES AND OTHER PROTESTS

Marches are obvious ways to show unity for a common cause. They often start or end with speeches, and marchers may chant slogans, sing songs, and carry placards with messages as they walk. These help attract attention and spread the marchers' message to the public wherever they pass, unlike a meeting that happens in one place. As marches are public, they also attract interest from the media, which can spread the message even further.

Marching was just one of the types of group direct action protests used by civil rights protestors. For example, in February 1960, four black students from North Carolina Agriculture and Technical College sat down in the white-only canteen at Greensboro Woolworth's store. They were refused service but remained sitting until closing time. The next morning they were joined by 20 more students, and the day after that 63 more. After five days, there were 300 protestors. After some students were arrested, **sit-in** protests spread to segregated canteens at many Woolworth's. After six months of sit-ins, sales had dropped by a third, forcing Woolworth's to end segregation.

FREEDOM RIDES

The **freedom rides** of May 1961 were another group direct action protest, this time against segregation on buses and in stations. Thirteen people – blacks and whites – boarded and sat together on two buses that set off from Washington, DC to stop off at towns and cities in the South. One bus was firebombed in Alabama, and riders were badly beaten with pipes and chains by white people furious at what they were doing. Some riders were arrested or hospitalized, but more riders joined the route. Images and reports of burning buses and beaten riders gained national attention.

One freedom rider, Hank Thomas, explained in an interview later how the riders expected trouble and why they travelled in smart clothes:

> [We were] well dressed, mannerly, orderly black folks just asking for what ordinary Americans were asking for. And the contrast between us and the mob was these white toughs who spoke poor English and everything about them seemed to say these are uneducated folks ... and we're the ones that are being refused service... We wanted that contrast to be there.

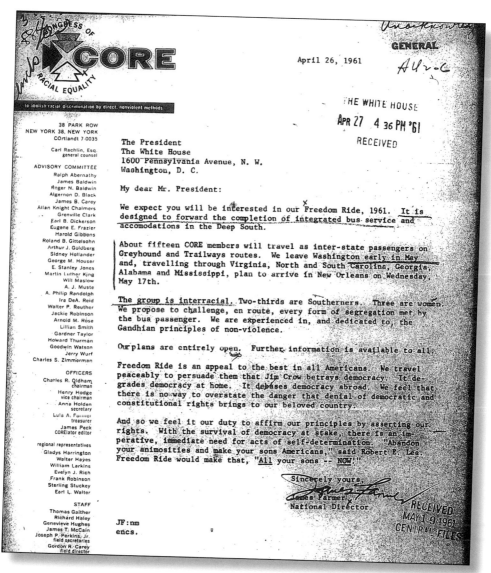

CONGRESS OF

CORE

RACIAL EQUALITY

to abolish racial discrimination by direct, nonviolent methods

GENERAL

April 26, 1961

38 PARK ROW
NEW YORK 38, NEW YORK
COrtlandt 7-0035

THE WHITE HOUSE

APR 27 4 36 PM '61

RECEIVED

Carl Rachlin, Esq.
general counsel

ADVISORY COMMITTEE
Ralph Abernathy
James Baldwin
Roger N. Baldwin
Algernon D. Black
James B. Carey
Allan Knight Chalmers
Grenville Clark
Earl B. Dickerson
Eugene E. Frazier
Harold Gibbons
Roland B. Gittelsohn
Arthur J. Goldberg
Sidney Hollander
George M. Houser
E. Stanley Jones
Martin Luther King
Will Maslow
A. J. Muste
A. Philip Randolph
Ira DeA. Reid
Walter P. Reuther
Jackie Robinson
Arnold M. Rose
Lillian Smith
Gardner Taylor
Howard Thurman
Goodwin Watson
Jerry Wurf
Charles S. Zimmerman

OFFICERS
Charles R. Oldham
chairman
Henry Hodge
vice chairman
Anna Holden
secretary
Lula A. Farmer
treasurer
James Peck
CORElator editor

regional representatives
Gladys Harrington
Walter Hayes
William Larkins
Evelyn J. Rich
Frank Robinson
Sterling Stuckey
Earl L. Walter

STAFF
Thomas Gaither
Richard Haley
Genevieve Hughes
James T. McCain
Joseph P. Perkins, Jr.
field secretaries
Gordon R. Carey
field director

The President
The White House
1600 Pennsylvania Avenue, N. W.
Washington, D. C.

My dear Mr. President:

We expect you will be interested in our Freedom Ride, 1961. It is designed to forward the completion of integrated bus service and accomodations in the Deep South.

About fifteen CORE members will travel as inter-state passengers on Greyhound and Trailways routes. We leave Washington early in May and, travelling through Virginia, North and South Carolina, Georgia, Alabama and Mississippi, plan to arrive in New Orleans on Wednesday, May 17th.

The group is interracial. Two-thirds are Southerners. Three are women. We propose to challenge, en route, every form of segregation met by the bus passenger. We are experienced in, and dedicated to, the Gandhian principles of non-violence.

Our plans are entirely open. Further information is available to all.

Freedom Ride is an appeal to the best in all Americans. We travel peaceably to persuade them that Jim Crow betrays democracy. It degrades democracy at home. It debases democracy abroad. We feel that there is no way to overstate the danger that denial of democratic and constitutional rights brings to our beloved country.

And so we feel it our duty to affirm our principles by asserting our rights. With the survival of democracy at stake, there is an imperative, immediate need for acts of self-determination. "Abandon your animosities and make your sons Americans," said Robert E. Lee. Freedom Ride would make that, "All your sons -- NOW!"

Sincerely yours,

James Farmer
National Director

JF:nm
encs.

RECEIVED
MAY 1 9 1961
CENTRAL FILES

▲ This primary source is the original letter from the freedom riders to the US President to announce their intention to confront segregation in the South.

AVOIDING VIOLENCE

One of the most important principles of the civil rights protests was that they should be non-violent. This meant that even if marchers were pushed, hit, spat at, or otherwise provoked, they should never fight back. Mohandas Gandhi was a great influence on some civil rights leaders such as Martin Luther King Jr. Gandhi had used non-violent protest against British rule to gain eventual independence for India. King was an increasingly important civil rights leader and therefore a target for violence from segregationists. However, during the boycotts, he chose not to have armed bodyguards for protection, but instead to face arrest and physical violence. He even reacted with compassion when extremists firebombed his home. King developed several key beliefs about non-violence:

- non-violence aims to gain understanding of your enemy
- you should expect to suffer for your cause
- non-violence is both in action and thought.

WHO IN HISTORY

MOHANDAS GANDHI
1869–1948
BORN: Porbandar, India

ROLE: Gandhi developed and popularized mass non-violent protest against British rulers in South Africa and India. For example, when Britain put a tax on salt, Gandhi walked hundreds of kilometres to the sea to make his own salt, which was illegal. Thousands of Indians joined him in his march, and many were arrested and treated badly but did not fight back. Gandhi led many non-violent protests like this, and they influenced protest movements worldwide.

Did You Know?

Even though he was famous and wealthy, Ghandi spun his own cotton cloth to make his clothing.

King was a **Baptist** Church leader in Montgomery, Alabama and talked about non-violent protests to his **congregation**. He joined with other black clergymen and civil rights protestors to form the **Southern Christian Leadership Conference (SCLC)**, which encouraged the use of non-violence in the southern US states. King said:

> Non-violence is a powerful and just weapon which cuts without wounding and ennobles the man who wields it. It is a sword that heals.

◀ Websites such as the Library of Congress Voices of Civil Rights pages provide invaluable collections of primary sources.

OTHER WAYS

Some civil rights marchers struggled with the idea that non-violence was the only way to protest, especially after witnessing or experiencing violence themselves. Rob Williams was an NAACP leader who lived in Monroe, North Carolina, where there was widespread persecution by the KKK of any black people trying to fight for civil rights. He grew frustrated by this and how white courts in the state did not give fair trials or protection to black people. Williams formed an armed group called the Black Guard, which was committed to the protection of Monroe's black population. In 1959, he said:

> It is time for [black] men to stand up and be men and if it is necessary for us to die we must be willing to die. If it is necessary for us to kill we must be willing to kill.

Malcolm X and those involved in the black power movement (see pages 48–49) also questioned non-violence in the early 1960s.

WHAT SORT OF PEOPLE WERE THEY?

In summer 2008, filmmaker Robin Fryday went to Alabama to research a documentary about surviving participants in civil rights marches and other protesters who lived there. She met many people who had taken part in marches. But one interviewee in Birmingham asked if she had met the barber. Fryday went to the shop she was directed to. "It's a tiny little barber shop, but every inch of space was covered with photographs and newspaper clippings and memorabilia from the civil rights movement ... the shop was almost like a living museum."

James Armstrong had been a barber in the city for 50 years after returning from fighting in World War II. He had carried a flag in a famous Selma to Montgomery march in 1965 (see pages 36–39). He had battled segregation in different ways, such as by getting his children into an all-white school and buying a home in a white neighbourhood.

◀ James Armstrong's barber shop was one of several focal points for civil rights discussions in the segregated city of Birmingham, Alabama during the 1950s and 1960s.

Over the years, Armstrong had chatted and debated with thousands of customers about civil rights and encouraged them to get involved in civil rights protests. He said: "If you want a voice, you have to vote; you can't complain about nothing if you don't vote... Dying isn't the worst thing a man can do. The worst thing a man can do is nothing."

Fryday used interviews with Armstrong as a central thread through her film, which went on to get an Oscar nomination. She said about him: "James Armstrong was so ordinary yet so extraordinary. As [Armstrong] says in the film, he wanted to live with a purpose, and I carry those words with me." Discover more about the film that Robin Fryday made at barberofbirmingham.com.

RANGE

Civil rights marchers came from all walks of life. For example, William Lewis Moore was a postal worker, Jackie Robinson was a famous retired baseball player, Fannie Hamer worked in cotton fields, Frederick Walbert was a music teacher, and Viola Liuzzo was a housewife. Most marchers were black, but some were white. Some were old, others were young. Sheyann Webb was just eight years old when she was inspired to march at Selma, Alabama in 1965, after hearing King talk at a church meeting. She felt very strongly about marching but was so scared that she wrote plans for her own funeral just in case!

HISTORY DETECTIVES: ORAL HISTORY

Have you ever listened to older people recalling when they were young? This is known as oral history. Some historians make recordings of oral history to capture such memories. When you are researching recent historical events, see if you can interview someone who was there. Plan what questions you want to ask – for example, don't ask about pets or hobbies if you are trying to find out more about protests. Remember to record in a place without background noise so that it does not spoil the recording.

STUDENTS

Diane Nash grew up in Chicago where there was no official segregation. When she went to university in Nashville in the late 1950s, she was shocked not only to experience segregation but also by the lack of interest on the campus about improving civil rights.

> I recall talking to a number of people in the dormitories at school and on campus, and asking them if they knew any people who were trying … to bring about some type of change. And I remember … getting almost depressed, because I encountered what I thought was so much apathy.

But universities were a major focus for the civil rights movement. From the mid-1950s onwards, more universities in the South were starting to desegregate. More white students met and spent time with black students on campus than before, and they grew angry about injustices in their country, including the infamous case of Emmett Till (see below). Students were becoming more interested in free speech and not automatically conforming to what society expected of them.

WHO IN HISTORY

EMMETT TILL
1941–1955
BORN: Chicago, Illinois

ROLE: Emmett Till was a black 14-year-old boy visiting relatives in Mississippi. He made the fatal mistake of being cheeky to a white woman, and was lynched. His body was thrown in a river. A court pronounced the men who admitted snatching him not guilty. The men later admitted to killing Till. Till's death and photos of his beaten body made many people in Northern cities realize the harshness of life for black people in the South.

Did You Know?
Emmett loved jokes so much that he paid people to tell them to him.

Some students became motivated to march after experiencing racism in the South. Others, such as John Lewis, grew up in the South. He was the son of poor black farmers in Alabama, so he knew about segregation at first hand. He was arrested and beaten many times as a freedom rider and went on to help co-ordinate marches across the United States. The students who became marchers were not just at Southern universities. Bob Moses grew up in New York and studied at Harvard University. He and other Northern students travelled to the South to try to encourage black people there to register to vote.

CANCELLED MARCH

Bayard Rustin was a student and teacher who was a major figure in the civil rights marches. In 1941, with A. Philip Randolph, he planned a march in Washington, DC to end segregation in arms factories. These factories were booming during World War II, but only white people could get jobs there. They called the march off after meeting US President Roosevelt, who changed laws to make it easier for black people to work in the factories. Randolph later organized the 1963 march (see pages 4–5 and 32–33).

▲ Civil rights activist and leader Bayard Rustin.

CHURCH COMMUNITY

The Baptist Church in the South was more than a place for black people to worship; it was also a centre of their community. The church helped people sort out disputes, financial problems, gave support to those in need, and was a place where marches were publicized. Many people became marchers after hearing speeches and singing songs in church.

Martin Luther King Jr, Fred Shuttlesworth, and Ralph Abernathy are amongst the most famous Baptist leaders who marched. King joined the movement after encouragement from organizers of the Montgomery Bus Boycotts. They knew that if King joined the boycott then so might many of his congregation. People in the civil rights movement knew that Baptist churches in the South were a safe haven for black people. In church, black people might be persuaded to have the courage to take direct action. Getting congregations onside could also help raise funds for the cause.

People from other faiths also marched. Abraham Joshua Heschel was a Jewish rabbi who was expelled from Germany during World War II and eventually settled in the United States. He walked arm in arm with King at the famous Selma–Montgomery marches (see pages 36–39). Heschel believed that marching was a religious activity – not only in showing compassion for the oppressed but also as a focus of prayer.

> For many of us the march from Selma to Montgomery was about protest and prayer. Legs are not lips and walking is not kneeling. And yet our legs uttered songs. Even without words, our march was worship. I felt my legs were praying.
Abraham Heschel

UNREST IN THE CHURCH

Religious protestors like any others faced hostilities from the white community and the Ku Klux Klan for supporting civil rights protests. But some also faced disapproval from their religious leaders. In 1963, Father Maurice Ouellet wrote to Catholic leader Archbishop Toolen to ask official permission for Ouellet and other members of his Catholic **mission** to participate in marches. Toolen was concerned that the association with unrest and violence would drive away worshippers from the church.

In response to Ouellet's request, Toolen wrote:

> *I won't stand for any priest ... going in parades or sit-ins ... the marches ... have done absolutely no good... Of course, you realize you are stirring up great trouble for yourself, as I have told you, Selma and the surrounding country as far as [black people are] concerned is and always has been the worst in the state. They hate [black people], and hate him worse than they love the Church.*

Ouellet did not march but instead offered food and assistance to marchers. This was enough for the Archbishop to send him away from his mission to another part of the United States.

▼ Baptist churches could become targets of attack. The 16th Street Baptist Church in Birmingham, Alabama, was the site of a racist bombing in 1963 in which four young girls died. It is now a national landmark in commemoration of the civil rights struggle.

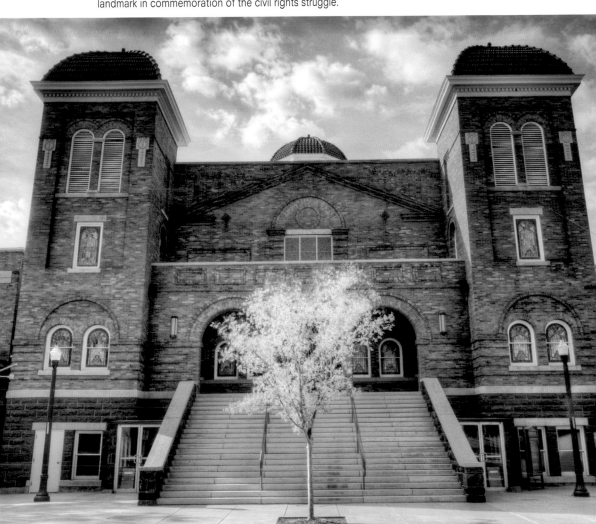

ORGANIZATIONS

Many marchers joined the protest because they were members of civil rights organizations. The main ones in the late 1950s to 1960s were the SCLC and the Student Nonviolent Coordinating Committee (SNCC). Julian Bond was a founding member of the SNCC. In an interview in 2010, he recalled why he joined their protests in the most segregated parts of the United States: "Because we were young ... we dared to take risks that our elders didn't take. They told us that in Mississippi, segregation could only be attacked from the outside, and we went right to the heart of the beast and attacked it there and beat it there."

THE FUTURE...

The future means redoubled efforts to continue . . .

—introducing educated and determined young workers into hard core areas;

—maintaining a college contact that leads to militant action in cities and provides new recruits for full time work.

The future means . . .

—expanding our pilot voter registration projects in cities to provide workers in surrounding counties.

—finding more funds to support students willing to work at subsistence wages and share the life of the Southern rural Negro while trying to convince him of his rights.

—providing more and better workshops and conferences on the meaning and techniques of nonviolent community action and political involvement.

Change will be slow, but change must take place. SNCC will need *three times our current staff* to do the job we have only begun. We will also need *three times our current budget*.

The future means your support . . .

—in contributions and in stimulating your local community to break down every form of racial discrimination now.

—in letting us know how we can help you and how you can help us.

DANVILLE, VA.

▲ This SNCC brochure states the aims of the organization.

HISTORY DETECTIVES:
NAVIGATING SOURCES

In your local library, you may find several books that mention civil rights. Some will be more useful than others. You can navigate books by using the contents or index pages, and locate relevant information for your research quickly by skim reading the headings and looking at the pictures.

On the internet, you may find millions of sources. One easy way to decide which ones to look at are the ends of website addresses. Those produced by governments end in .gov and educational organizations end in .edu. These may be less biased than commercial sites ending in .com.

WATCHING EYE

The US government was concerned that civil rights protestors might encourage unrest and violence. It kept an eye on marchers using its intelligence agency, the **FBI**. Some FBI agents secretly joined civil rights organizations and marches. Others paid or threatened marchers to pass on information.

In 2012, researcher Dr Christopher Phelps was looking at documents from during the civil rights march years on the FBI website. He discovered in a letter that an unnamed man "currently employed by the NAACP as a labor relations official" had been "contacted on several occasions by New York Agents and has been cooperative". Through research, he discovered that the NAACP official was called Herbert Hill. Hill had helped the FBI locate political radicals, who they then intimidated or arrested. As Phelps says: "It is [ironic] that an official dedicated to civil rights ... could simultaneously provide assistance in naming names that would [reduce] political and civil liberties."

WHERE DID PEOPLE MARCH?

On 2 May 1963, in Birmingham, Alabama, a big civil rights march was about to begin. Police had massed around a park by the 16th Street Baptist Church. Thousands of black people looked on. Inside the church, there were 2,000 protestors. Len Holt was a reporter who witnessed what happened next:

"Freedom! Freedom!" A roar arose from the church. The cops almost as one, faced the church. Some unleashed clubs from their belts. The faces of those I could see had turned crimson... Before I could get back to the motel the demonstrations began; 60 demonstrators were on their way, marching two abreast, each with a sign bearing an integration slogan. Dick Gregory, the nightclub comedian, was leading the group. At a signal, 40 policemen converged, sticks in hand. Up drove yellow school buses...

"Do you have a permit to parade?" asked the police captain.

"No," replied Gregory.

"No what?" asked the captain in what seemed to be a reminder to Gregory that he had not used a "sir."

"No. No. A thousand times No," Gregory replied.

The captain said, "I hereby place you all under arrest for parading without a permit, disturbing the peace and violating the injunction of the Circuit Court of Jefferson County..."

And for the next two hours this scene was repeated over and over as group after group of students strutted out of the church to the cheers of the spectators, the freedom chants of those being carried away in buses and a continuous banging on the floors and sides of the buses.

THE RIGHT PLACE TO PROTEST

Civil rights marches happened in many places across the United States, from the capital Washington, DC to places facing extreme segregation in the South (see map on page 34). March organizers chose Birmingham in 1963 for several reasons:

- Its population contained a high percentage of black people, and one of its most popular church leaders, Fred Shuttlesworth, strongly supported the civil rights protest. Protests would have many supporters.
- It was the most segregated large city in the South and known as "Bombingham" because there had been so many firebombings of churches and homes of prominent black activists.
- Its Public Safety Commissioner Eugene "Bull" Connor was well known for ordering rough treatment of civil rights protestors.

Organizers informed the Birmingham authorities to expect a march and invited the media to attend. They did not predict how extreme the response of Connor and his men would be on 3 May. Photos and reports of non-violent black protestors knocked down by high-pressure water from fire hoses and attacked by police dogs appeared in newspapers and on TV worldwide. This angered the public and helped to raise awareness of and support for the civil rights movement.

◀ Marcher Walter Gadsden is attacked by police dogs in Birmingham, Alabama. The police were attempting to clear peaceful civil rights protestors from the streets.

MARCH TACTICS

Once they had chosen where to march, civil rights marchers used different tactics to try to make their protests count. For example, the Birmingham march was preceded by a month of other protests as part of the Birmingham Campaign that gained little publicity. At the start of May, campaign organizers, including Fred Shuttlesworth, James Bevel, and Martin Luther King Jr, decided a change in tactics was necessary. Bevel realized that fewer black adults were marching because they risked arrest and would then probably lose their jobs. Jobs with reasonable pay for black people were uncommon in segregated Birmingham. Bevel came up with the idea of encouraging schoolchildren to march instead to increase numbers without risking jobs. These marches became known as the Children's Crusades. Waves of children marched from the church to different shops and other sites in Birmingham, which they occupied until they were moved on or arrested. In total, 2,000 children were arrested.

Not everyone agreed with Bevel's controversial tactic, saying it put children in danger. Some teachers even tried to stop children leaving school buildings on march days, although some escaped through classroom windows! Despite some people's reservations, the Children's Crusades created great media attention and highlighted the striking contrast between non-violent child protestors and armed adult police.

▼ Young black protestors huddle and protect each other from high-pressure water jets directed by firefighters trying to break up the Birmingham march in May 1963.

Another tactic was to use King's high profile as a civil rights leader to gain more attention. King toured US cities before the Birmingham Campaign to raise funds. Organizers anticipated that King would be arrested by Connor and his police, and rapidly spread news of his arrest across the United States. They then did not pay the sum of money necessary to get King out of prison immediately. This ensured that there was more media coverage of his arrest and imprisonment for peaceful protest.

WHO IN HISTORY

FRED SHUTTLESWORTH
1922–2011
BORN: Mount Meigs, Alabama

ROLE: Shuttlesworth helped found the SCLC and co-led the Children's Crusades in Birmingham. He was a lorry driver and cement worker who became a powerful preacher and joined the NAACP. The NAACP was banned in Alabama in 1956, but Shuttlesworth set up a Christian human rights organization to help black people before getting involved in the SCLC. He was beaten and bombed many times as a result. He invited King to come to the city to help bring change.

Did You Know?

Shuttlesworth was unhurt after his opponents exploded dynamite outside his bedroom as he lay in bed!

REPORTING CIVIL RIGHTS MARCHES

"A ... mother wept in the street Sunday morning in front of a Baptist Church in Birmingham. In her hand she held a shoe, one shoe, from the foot of her dead child. We hold that shoe with her...

Only we can trace the truth, Southerner – you and I. We broke those children's bodies. ...

We – who go on electing politicians who heat the kettles of hate...

We, who know better, created a climate for child-killing by those who don't."

Gene Patterson

This powerful piece appeared in the *Atlanta Constitution* newspaper on 16 September 1963 after the bombing of a church in Birmingham in which four young girls died. This was just a few months after the Children's Crusades. Some reporters on Southern city papers, such as Gene Patterson, had great sympathy for civil rights protesters, but not all papers printed such pieces. This was partly to protect their offices and reporters from being targeted by the KKK. Many newspapers in the 1950s and 1960s gave sparse accounts of civil rights marches and violence, using only basic information sent out by local newspaper offices. However, the *New York Times* devoted lots of reporters, time, and money to the civil rights marches and regularly gave front-page space to the stories. This newspaper helped make civil rights a high priority political issue for the US government.

CAPTURING MARCHES

Photographers working for newspapers and magazines captured thousands of images of the civil rights marches. Some, such as those of hoses being fired at children in Birmingham, the face of a beaten protester, or marchers whose route is blocked by armed soldiers, have become iconic. This means they represent something more than just the events they are showing. The Birmingham marchers, for example, represent all innocent or powerless people targeted by troops or other people in a position of power. They also remind us of the imbalance in power faced and challenged by civil rights protestors. Iconic images helped make many viewers support the civil rights cause.

▲ Here you can see demonstrators in Birmingham, Alabama shouting and jeering at the cameraman and the police. See below for how pictures can tell different stories.

HISTORY DETECTIVES:
INTERPRETING A PHOTO

A photo of an event in a newspaper is rarely objective. It is usually subjective because a photographer, or the publication that printed the image, made choices about what to show and what to leave out to complement a story. Take care in researching photos. For example, contrast the photo on page 27 of the boy calmly facing a dog attack with the one above. Both were taken at the same event in Birmingham. Either viewed alone might make us think very differently about the behaviour and attitude of the demonstrators and the police.

IN WASHINGTON

Many groups have organized mass marches in Washington, DC because it is the seat of US government. The first civil rights event planned in the city was the 1941 March for Jobs. In 1963, the same organizers, A. Philip Randolph and Bayard Rustin, realized that it was again time for a big march in the capital. They knew that the massive publicity for recent events in Birmingham, Alabama, would guarantee high attendance and media interest. This was the March on Washington for Jobs and Freedom.

Rustin put together an organizing team. They raised money for the march by selling badges and collecting contributions from people and groups sympathetic to their cause. They organized celebrities to attend, such as actors Sidney Poitier and Marlon Brando, and entertainers Harry Belafonte and Sammy Davis Jr. They made publicity posters and leaflets, and planned transport for protestors travelling from as far afield as Alabama and Arkansas. See the official program for the 1963 march at www. ourdocuments.gov/doc.php?flash=true&doc=96.

▼ Several famous stars turned up to support the cause and attract more protestors at the Washington, DC march. They included (front, from left to right) actor Charlton Heston, writer James Baldwin, actor Marlon Brando, and singer Harry Belafonte.

LOCATION

Organizers wanted to march on Capitol Hill, but the government opposed this as it was close to the **White House**. They suggested assembling by the Washington Monument and not marching at all. Negotiations between the two sides resulted in a march from this assembly point to the nearby Lincoln Memorial. This monument was symbolic for black people because Abraham Lincoln was the president who had played a major role in **emancipation** of slaves in the 19th century. But a large pool in front of the Memorial meant there was not much space. Organizers had planned for 150,000 protestors, but estimated that nearly twice this number turned up.

MARCH ON WASHINGTON FOR JOBS AND FREEDOM
AUGUST 28, 1963

LINCOLN MEMORIAL PROGRAM

1.	The National Anthem	Led by Marian Anderson.
2.	Invocation	The Very Rev. Patrick O'Boyle, Archbishop of Washington.
3.	Opening Remarks	A. Philip Randolph, Director March on Washington for Jobs and Freedom.
4.	Remarks	Dr. Eugene Carson Blake, Stated Clerk, United Presbyterian Church of the U.S.A.; Vice Chairman, Commission on Race Relations of the National Council of Churches of Christ in America.
5.	Tribute to Negro Women Fighters for Freedom Daisy Bates Diane Nash Bevel Mrs. Medgar Evers Mrs. Herbert Lee Rosa Parks Gloria Richardson	Mrs. Medgar Evers
6.	Remarks	John Lewis, National Chairman, Student Nonviolent Coordinating Committee.
7.	Remarks	Walter Reuther, President, United Automobile, Aerospace and Agricultural Implement Wokers of America, AFL-CIO; Chairman, Industrial Union Department, AFL-CIO.
8.	Remarks	James Farmer, National Director, Congress of Racial Equality.
9.	Selection	Eva Jessye Choir
10.	Prayer	Rabbi Uri Miller, President Synagogue Council of America.
11.	Remarks	Whitney M. Young, Jr., Executive Director, National Urban League.
12.	Remarks	Mathew Ahmann, Executive Director, National Catholic Conference for Interracial Justice.
13.	Remarks	Roy Wilkins, Executive Secretary, National Association for the Advancement of Colored People.
14.	Selection	Miss Mahalia Jackson
15.	Remarks	Rabbi Joachim Prinz, President American Jewish Congress.
16.	Remarks	The Rev. Dr. Martin Luther King, Jr., President, Southern Christian Leadership Conference.
17.	The Pledge	A Philip Randolph
18.	Benediction	Dr. Benjamin E. Mays, President, Morehouse College.

"WE SHALL OVERCOME"

▲ This primary source is the programme of events for the famous march on Washington, DC at the Lincoln Memorial in 1963.

DIVIDED OPINIONS

Protestors present on the day could not agree over whether the Washington, DC event achieved its goals. SNCC executive Avon Rollins said: "I was awestruck by the multi-colored faces of the marchers… We all were joined together that day, equalized by our purpose for social and economic change in America. I felt that I was truly an eyewitness to history."

But some members of the SNCC had wanted to use the day for disruption in Washington, DC, such as jamming telephone lines in government buildings and chaining themselves to the White House. SNCC organizer Julius Lester said: "The March was nothing but a giant therapy session that allowed Dr. King to [speak] about his dreams of a [black man] eating at the same table with some [Southern white person], while most black folks just dreamed about eating."

MARCHING ORDERS

Organizers carefully controlled the march on Washington, DC in a variety of ways. They had a list of official demands to make to the government. These included making new laws guaranteeing all Americans decent housing, adequate and integrated education, the right to vote, and a fair minimum wage. To make sure that government heard the speeches, organizers invited every congressman and senator to the Lincoln Memorial at 12.00 on the day. Organizers insisted that marchers only carried banners with slogans that they provided. These represented the official demands of the march to help onlookers understand why protestors were marching.

Many other practical details were planned, too. Marchers were asked to bring packed lunches as many city centre shops were closed on the day of the march. Spouts were attached to fire hydrants so marchers would have access to drinking water on or near the marching route. Organizers requested that every bus or train bringing marchers to Washington, DC had a "captain" or person responsible for the welfare and discipline of marchers. Over 2,000 volunteer marshals who were members of the SNCC or other groups were on hand to help direct marchers.

▼ These are the sights of some of the most famous civil rights marches and protests.

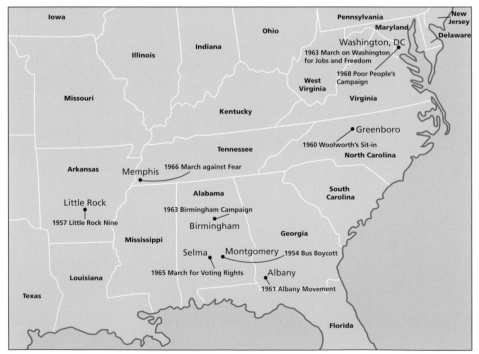

POLITICAL CHANGE

The march on Washington, DC and civil rights protests staged across the South spurred the US government to make a change. President Kennedy was **assassinated** before his proposed changes to civil rights laws had been approved by the government. This took over a year because Southerners argued the bill would affect the rights of individuals and states in making their own laws. In 1964, President Lyndon Johnson finally pushed through the **Civil Rights Act**, banning segregation in public places and in employment on the grounds of race or religious beliefs. Jim Crow laws about segregation were overturned, and within a few years, most signs saying "Colored" or "White-Only" were removed across the South. However, unofficial segregation did persist, and the new focus of marches was to make it possible for more black people to vote so they could choose who represented them in government.

Think About This

Would better technology have helped?

In 2011 and 2012, there were political protests in countries across North Africa and the Middle East. News about them spread fast partly because of protest organizers using social media such as Twitter and Facebook. Do you think the civil rights changes would have happened more quickly with better technology?

CIVIL RIGHTS MARCHES

Where	When	Number marching	How far they marched
Albany Movement: Albany, Georgia	1961	2,000	1.6 kilometres (1 mile)
Birmingham Campaign: Birmingham, Alabama	May 1963	6,000	1.6 kilometres (1 mile)
March on Washington for Jobs and Freedom: Washington, DC	August 1963	200,000	1.6 kilometres (1 mile)
March for Voting Rights: Selma–Montgomery, Alabama	1965	600–25,000	80 kilometres (50 miles)
March against Fear: Memphis, Tennessee to Jackson, Mississippi	1966	1 initially, growing to 15,000	354 kilometres (220 miles)
Poor People's March: Washington, DC	1968	3,000	1.6 kilometres (1 mile)

WHAT HAPPENED TO PEOPLE ON THE MARCHES?

On the morning of 7 March 1965, a group of marchers left the Brown Chapel African Methodist Episcopal Church in Selma. Their aim was to stage a march from Selma to Montgomery, the Alabama state capital. They wanted to protest primarily about black people not being able to vote in the state, but also about the death of a marcher called Jimmie Lee Jackson in the previous month. Many were dressed in Sunday best clothes and planned to walk only part of the 80-kilometre (50-mile) route to show their support. But the SCLC marchers and organizers knew that the state police, led by Sheriff Jim Clark, would try to stop them. One of the marchers was Amelia Boynton. In an interview in the 1980s, she described what she saw on the outskirts of the town:

> Just before we got to the light across the [Edmund Pettus] bridge, we saw that the road was blocked. I didn't think anything was going to happen, but as we approached, it was announced, "Don't go any farther." And when Hosea Williams said, "May I say something?" Clark said, "No, you may not say anything. Charge on them, men!" And they started beating us. They had horses. And I saw them when they were beating people down, and I just stood. Then one guy hit me with … a nightstick just back of the head and down toward the shoulder. And I still stood up there. Then the second [strike] was at the base of the neck. And I fell...

BLOODY SUNDAY

The day of this first Selma to Montgomery march came to be called **Bloody Sunday**. Around 200 police and state troopers, plus an armed group put together by the sheriff, charged the 600 marchers on horses, hitting out with truncheons, plastic tubing wrapped in barbed wire, and whips. The officers wore gas masks and exploded **tear gas** bombs in the crowd. Tear gas makes people choke and their eyes run uncontrollably. The officers beat the protestors while they were struggling with the effects of the gas. They even chased, whipped, and hit injured protestors trying to retreat to the church. Injuries included deep cuts, broken teeth, fractured ribs, and concussion. This is how the *New York Times* reported on Bloody Sunday: www.nytimes.com/packages/html/books/mlk-rout.pdf.

The violence against marchers horrified the nation. When the marchers regrouped two days later, supporters arriving in Selma swelled their numbers. They marched again, but this time the event was more symbolic. They went to the bridge, knelt, and prayed for the injured in view of the waiting police, state troopers, and onlookers, including reporters. The second march is often called Turnaround Tuesday. Just under two weeks later, an even larger group marched. But on this third and final march, the marchers had government protection from racist violence, including armed National Guards, and made it to Montgomery.

▼ The three Selma to Montgomery marches went through several Alabama counties where black people were denied the right to vote.

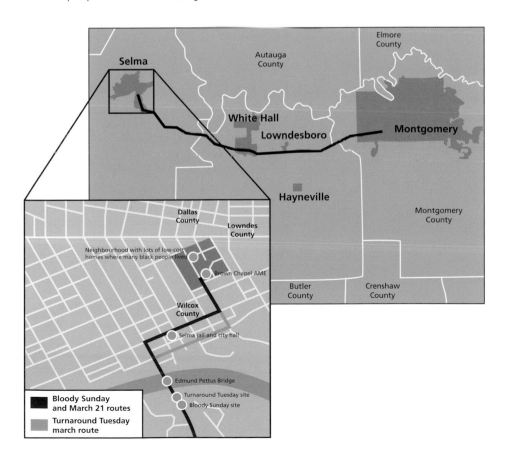

ILL TREATMENT

*People used to tickle me, talking about how brave I was …
marching … because I was so scared. All the time. It was like
wall-to-wall terrified. I can remember sitting in class, many times,
before demonstrations, and I knew, like, we were going to have a
demonstration that afternoon. And the palms of hands would be so
sweaty, and I would be so tense and tight inside. I was really afraid.*
Diane Nash

This quote by Diane Nash shows how she knew that protesting for civil
rights was dangerous. Protestors could expect ill treatment, especially in
places in the South where there were many people fiercely against an end
to segregation as well as aggressive troops and officers upholding local
laws. The hostilities could be verbal such as name-calling. Physical violence
ranged from slapping and shoving to beatings with anything from sticks
to electric cattle prods. In Birmingham, Alabama, the water from hoses
directed at marchers was powerful enough to rip the bark from trees. It
knocked protestors down and caused bruising or even internal bleeding.

▼ Martin Luther King Jr (fifth from the right) leads civil rights activists
from Selma to Montgomery.

HISTORY DETECTIVES: TIMELINES

During research into a historical topic, you may end up with lots of information. Organize this information into a timeline so that it is easier to understand. Timelines help establish the order of events in a period of history. They can be at different scales, for example, by month and year or by day during one month.

Timeline of the Selma marches

7 March: Bloody Sunday: first and most violent march at Selma. Around 50 of the 600 marchers were injured by troops and police officers soon after setting off.

9 March: Turnaround Tuesday: 2,000 marchers stopped before the Pettus bridge to pray for the victims before returning to Selma.

21 March: Selma to Montgomery: Thousands marched over 80 kilometres (50 miles) to Montgomery, escorted and protected by troops sent in by President Johnson.

TESTING NON-VIOLENCE

Civil rights organizations told protestors not to hit back at aggressive segregationists, but it was not always easy to remain non-violent. On Bloody Sunday, at least one police officer was injured by retreating protestors throwing bricks. A few months earlier, Annie Lee Cooper had been waiting to register as a voter when Sheriff Clark poked her in the neck with his truncheon, twisted her arm, and tried to force her home. She punched Clark, almost knocking him over, and his response was to hit her on the head hard with his truncheon and throw her into prison. Some people praised her for taking a beating on their behalf. But civil rights leader James Bevel said **retaliation** did not help the cause because: "Then [the press] don't talk about the registration. We want the world to know they ain't registering nobody!"

You can see reports of people injured by police on the Birmingham march in 1963 on www.archives.state.al.us/teacher/rights/lesson3/doc6.html.

ANTICIPATING REACTION

Organizers told marchers what to expect during their protests. They expected to be arrested as they would be breaking many laws by marching. For example, Selma courts made a ruling in 1964 that if five or more people were found congregating on the streets discussing the right to vote, they would be arrested. King ordered the return to Selma on Turnaround Tuesday because he did not want to anger a white judge sympathetic to the civil rights cause who was in the process of overturning this law. Marchers were also trained in how to protect themselves if they were attacked. Diane Nash recalls training classes when she was a student:

> We would practice things such as how to protect your head from a beating, how to protect each other, if one person was taking a severe beating, we would practice other people putting their bodies in between that person and the violence. So that the violence could be more distributed and hopefully no one would get seriously injured. We would practice not striking back, if someone struck us.

◀ "[Sheriff] Jim Clark couldn't see from the other movements that what he was doing to us was not only playing into our hands but going to bring the nation down on him." Hosea Williams, National Director of Voter Registration and Political Education for the SCLC, 1965

PREVENTED FROM VOTING

In 1870, the US Constitution included in its 15th Amendment that no citizen should be denied the right to vote based on race or colour. Yet in the early 1960s, most black people were still denied this right in the South. This was because state governments used a range of restrictions on who could vote: people could vote only if they passed tests proving their knowledge, if their grandfather had voted in the past before 1867, if they owned property, or if they could pay a poll tax. These restrictions excluded most black people who were poor, lacked education, and whose grandparents had often been in slavery. Also, the major political party in the South, the Democratic Party, only allowed white members. The restrictions meant that of those eligible to vote in the South, very few were officially registered to do so. The table shows **voter registration** in three counties of Alabama in 1964, before the Selma–Montgomery marches:

	Lowndes Co.	Dallas Co.	Perry Co.
Percentage of population that was black and over 21	70	51	60
Percentage of registered black voters	0	2	5

The successful Selma march culminated in a final rally of some 25,000 people by the steps of the capitol building in central Montgomery. King gave a stirring speech:

> They told us we wouldn't get here. And there were those who said that we would get here only over their dead bodies but all the world today knows that we are here and we are standing before the forces of power in the state of Alabama saying, "We ain't goin' let nobody turn us around."

He and other march leaders took a petition demanding changes to voting laws to the offices of state governor Wallace but he refused to meet them. Nevertheless it was clear that the end to voting segregation in the state was near.

GOING FURTHER

Some people were killed for taking part in civil rights protests. Murders were most numerous in the South, notably Mississippi, and many were a result of efforts of people to increase the number of black people registered to vote. For example, white racists murdered Reverend George Lee when he refused to take his name off a list of registered voters, and Herbert Lee was killed for attending classes about voter education.

▼ Two Alabama state troopers stand near the car in which Viola Liuzzo (see page 43) was murdered by members of the Ku Klux Klan.

Many protestors and their families also faced long-lasting retaliation from people opposing equal rights. For example, the principals of Birmingham schools were told to expel Children's Crusaders in 1963, and in 1964, Mississippi State authorities stopped food relief for poor people who wanted to register as voters, so families did not have enough to eat. Many protestors' businesses were destroyed or harmed, for example by firebombing, by being refused loans at banks, or having deliveries of goods stopped.

MARCH DEATHS IN ALABAMA

The Selma marches were framed by several tragic deaths of protestors at the hands of those who violently opposed segregation.

Jimmie Lee Jackson: On the night of 17 February, a night march from Selma to nearby Marion ended in tragedy. Jimmie Lee Jackson was shot and killed by police as he tried to protect his mother, whom the police were beating. This created outrage in the black community but was not reported widely in the national media. Organizer Jim Bevel said, "it would be fitting to take Jimmie Lee's body and march it all the way to the state capitol in Montgomery." This was what prompted the first Selma to Montgomery march.

James Reeb: Reeb was a white minister from Boston who had come to Selma to march. On the night of Turnaround Tuesday, Reeb and two black companions strayed into an area of town where local black people would normally never go. Reeb was hit with a club by a white man and refused treatment at the Selma hospital. He died on the way to a Birmingham hospital. This death caused national outrage. Stokely Carmichael of the SNCC said: "What you want is the nation to be upset when anybody is killed ... but it almost [seems that] for this to be recognized, a white person must be killed."

Viola Liuzzo: Liuzzo took part in the successful third march on Montgomery. Afterwards, she offered to take marchers to Montgomery airport in a car with her black friend. Four KKK members spotted Viola, who was white, with her friend. They drove alongside the car and shot Liuzzo dead. This was a reminder to the marchers that despite their success in the third march, there was still a long battle to be fought.

PROTEST MUSIC

One cannot describe the … emotion this one song evokes across the Southland. I have heard it sung in great mass meetings with a thousand voices singing as one… I've heard the students singing it as they were being dragged away to jail. It generates power that is indescribable.

Wyatt T. Walker

Wyatt T. Walker, an SCLC leader, was talking about the song "We Shall Overcome", the unofficial anthem of the civil rights movement. Many protestors, especially those in the SCLC, were used to singing traditional hymns and **gospel** songs in black churches. They also sang a lot while marching, often in time with the walking pace. Some songs even had words about marching:

Onward, Christian soldiers
Marching as to war…

But marchers sang many different types of music, not just church music. These included popular soul or blues songs of the day such as "I Wish I Knew (How it would feel to be free)" by Nina Simone, "This Little Light of Mine" by Sam Cooke, and Curtis Mayfield's "Keep on Pushing", written after the Washington, DC march.

Civil rights leaders knew that singing together was important for marchers because it created unity in the cause. This is why they often organized concerts at meetings and rallies featuring professional musicians. Some of these performers grew more famous and spread civil rights songs to a much wider audience as a result. These included the gospel singer Mahalia Jackson, who sang before many of King's speeches. Jackson was an SCLC organizer who described what was special about her singing:

When there is no gap between what you say and who you are, what you say and what you believe – when you can express that in song, it is all the more powerful.

You can listen to some recordings of civil rights songs from the 1960s at www.teachersdomain.org/asset/iml04_vid_music.

▲ Nina Simone wrote the song "Mississippi Goddam" after feeling incensed by the murder of Medgar Evers and the Birmingham church bombing in 1963. The song was banned by several radio stations but popular amongst civil rights activists.

HIDDEN MESSAGE

In 2005, Robert Darden, a music historian, started the Black Gospel Music Restoration Project. He found old **singles** from the civil rights protest years, converted the music to digital files, and catalogued them into an archive to preserve the work. Darden discovered that the A-sides of records usually had a Christian message, but the B-sides called for support for the civil rights movement. For example, The Friendly Four's "Pray Before the Storm Comes" had a B-side called "Where is Freedom?", which has lyrics about marches, demonstrations in Birmingham, integration, violence, and snapping police dogs. Darden says, "Few radio stations, which mainly were white-owned, were … playing gospel music at all, so [the records] were not widely circulated. And what was on the B-side mostly was being listened to in the black community. It was a kind of private message."

VOTING RIGHTS

What happened on Bloody Sunday and the restraint shown by marchers on Turnaround Tuesday encouraged President Johnson to pressure Congress into changing voting rights laws. He knew that if he did not act fast then more people would be hurt. This could affect government popularity, which was already low because he had decided to call up US citizens to fight in the **Vietnam War**. On 6 August, with King and other civil rights leaders watching, Johnson signed the **Voting Rights Act 1965**. This prohibited stopping any US citizen from voting based on their race or colour, and abolished voting restrictions. Within months, black voter registration had risen dramatically in the South. But these were the last big civil rights protests that mobilized large numbers of both black and white people in a common cause.

WHO IN HISTORY

LYNDON JOHNSON
1908–1973

BORN: Stonewall, Texas

ROLE: As US president, Johnson pushed through both the Civil Rights Act in 1964 (and its amendment in 1968) and the Voting Rights Act of 1965. His pro-civil rights beliefs lost him the support of many people in the Democratic Party in Southern states. He also led the US into a large-scale war in Vietnam.

Did You Know?

As a young man, Johnson was a teacher in a segregated Mexican school in Texas.

RIOT AND LAST MARCH

In 1965, there was a major race riot in Watts, Los Angeles, sparked by the arrest of a black driver by a white police officer. Cars were burned and shops smashed and looted mostly by black residents. Over 10,000 National Guards were called in to restore order; 34 people were killed and thousands arrested. King and many other civil rights leaders knew that such violence would reduce nationwide approval for civil rights protests. They turned their attention towards the root causes of unrest and riots in Northern US cities. These included poor housing and low-paid jobs. King helped organize a Poor People's Campaign, including a march on Washington, DC to demand, for example, a higher minimum wage. However, before the march took place, King was assassinated. You can read press reports about the Poor People's Campaign at www.pbs.org/wgbh/amex/eyesontheprize/story/15_poor.html.

The last significant civil rights march took place after King's death and was led by his widow Coretta Scott King, but it was not a success. Marchers were to walk to central Washington, DC and stay in a settlement of plywood shacks called Resurrection City on parkland. But the campaign soon started to run out of funds for building. New SCLC leader Ralph Abernathy negotiated with police to not arrest too many demonstrators because of low turnout. After six weeks, the campaign's permit for staying on the park ran out and National Guards closed Resurrection City.

▼ President Johnson (right) meets Martin Luther King Jr in the White House in 1966. The president was a champion of the civil rights movement.

WHAT HAPPENED TO MARCHERS AFTERWARDS?

This is the 27th time I have been arrested, and I ain't going to jail no more!... We want black power! That's right... We don't have to be ashamed of it... We've begged the federal government – that's all we've been doing, begging and begging. It's time we stand up and take over. Every courthouse in Mississippi ought to be burned down tomorrow to get rid of the dirt and the mess. From now on, when they ask you what you want, you know what to tell 'em. What do you want? Black power.

Stokely Carmichael

BLACK POWER

These are the words of Stokely Carmichael of the SNCC after being arrested during the 1966 March Against Fear in Mississippi. This march had been organized as a lone march by James Meredith, but Carmichael and Martin Luther King Jr took over after Meredith was shot and injured.

THE BLACK PANTHER PARTY

The Black Panther Party was founded in California by students Huey Newton and Bobby Seale. The group had a list of ten goals for their party, including giving every black person the land and property originally promised to their slave ancestors at the time of emancipation, and ending police brutality. View the party's Ten Point Platform at depts.washington.edu/civilr/display.cgi?image=bpp/docs/BPP4-8.jpg. Members wore black leather jackets and berets and carried guns, which were often not loaded. The government described the Panthers as government enemy number one, yet the party helped many poor black communities in California and Chicago, for example by giving out food and providing health care.

Carmichael joined the **Black Panther Party** soon after and his phrase "black power" became famous in the late 1960s. It symbolized a change of attitude amongst some civil rights protestors.

Many black people were deeply frustrated that the United States was spending billions of dollars overseas on the Vietnam War when many Americans were living in poverty. People like Carmichael said that non-violence was not working and that only the threat of violence could bring about social change in the United States. They also said that black people should be more independent of white people. The SCLC accused Carmichael of being a black racist. Infighting in the Black Panther Party and other groups about leadership and tactics, and prevention of their activities by the FBI, ended the black power movement in the 1970s.

INTO GOVERNMENT

Other civil rights protesters used the political skills they had developed through taking part in and organizing marches to eventually become representatives in government. Jesse Jackson had been a close colleague of King's, and went on to become a senior Democratic Party member. In 1986, John Lewis of the SNCC was elected to represent Georgia in the US House of Representatives.

▲ Controversially, sprinter Tommie Smith gave the black power salute during the 200-metres medal ceremony at the 1968 Olympic Games in Mexico.

OTHER CAUSES

Some marchers shifted their focus from the civil rights of black people to those of other groups. March organizer and protestor Bayard Rustin went on to defend Jewish people persecuted in the Soviet Union and campaigned for **gay rights** in the United States. Rustin was forced to leave the SCLC because he was gay. In 1986, he said: "The [test] of where one is on human rights questions is no longer the black community, it's the gay community … the community which is most easily mistreated."

Audrey Hendricks was one of the Children's Crusaders in Birmingham who was arrested for two weeks when she was eight. Hendricks went on to college in Texas and worked with children in residential centres who had emotional problems. The singer Harry Belafonte used his fame to encourage the support of stars for civil rights marches. He has since used this influence to support campaigns against HIV/AIDS, inequalities in world education, and world hunger. Belafonte is a goodwill ambassador for the global UNICEF organization that helps the children of the world. In 2012, he said: "Civil rights is a not a movement; it's a way of life. I'm saddened when I hear people say that the movement is over, for nothing could be further from the truth."

HISTORY DETECTIVES:
BIOGRAPHIES AND AUTOBIOGRAPHIES

Many civil rights marchers wrote autobiographies or feature in biographies. You can see a selection at multcolib.org/homework-center/civil-rights-biographies. Biographies can be fascinating summaries of lives and use primary sources within them. Autobiographies are primary sources.

Both types of source can have historical inaccuracies. An author may create an autobiography that presents them in a favourable way at the expense of getting all the facts right. Whatever sources you use for research, it is a good idea to double check key dates and facts against at least one other source.

H: This is an interview with Audrey Faye Hendricks for the Birmingham Civil Rights Institute's Oral History Project. I am Dr. Horace Huntley. We are at Miles College. Today is June 1, 1995.

       Welcome, Ms. Hendricks.

HE: Thank you.

H: Thank for taking time out of your schedule to come and sit with us today. I would just want to start by asking you some general kinds of questions about your family. Where are your parents from? Are they originally from Birmingham?

HE: My mother is from Birmingham -- is a native Birminghamian. My father is a native of Boligee, Alabama which is in Greene County.

H: I see. Where were you born?

HE: I was born in Birmingham.

H: How many brothers and sisters are there?

HE: There are two of us. I am the oldest of two girls.

H: Tell me just a bit about the education of your parents. How much schooling did they have.

HE: My mother finished Booker T. Washington Business College and my father did not complete elementary school, being in a rural township.

H: What were their occupations?

HE: My father was a laborer. He worked for Jim Dandy at the time and my mother worked for Alexander and Company with a black insurance company at that time doing clerical kinds of things.

H: Tell me about your education. Where did you start school? Did you start at Center Street?

HE: I started at Center Street. I went there for four years. And after the four years I went to

▲ This primary source is the transcript of an interview with Audrey Hendricks conducted by Horace Huntley on 1st June 1995.

WHAT DIFFERENCE DID I MAKE?

Other protesters questioned whether the marches had been as successful as they could have been. Prathia Hall was present on Bloody Sunday and what she saw made her lose some faith in non-violent protest. She later said, "We might have had even greater power if we had somehow found a way to allow space for the expression of righteous anger".

WHY WERE THE MARCHES SIGNIFICANT?

In 2008, the US public elected its first black president, Barack Obama. This is a stunning example of the significance of the civil rights marches in transforming US politics. The marches helped bring in the Voting Rights Act, which gradually increased the number of black representatives in government. The first senior black US diplomats included Colin Powell and Condoleeza Rice who were secretaries of state under President George W. Bush. In his inaugural address of 2013, Obama said:

> We, the people, declare today that the most evident of truths – that all of us are created equal – is the star that guides us still; just as it guided our forebears through … Selma…; just as it guided all those men and women, sung and unsung, who [marched] … to hear [Martin Luther King Jr] proclaim that our individual freedom is [tightly] bound to the freedom of every soul on Earth.

The success of non-violent marches in improving civil rights has meant it has become a protest tactic other groups have used to increase awareness of their cause. In 1970, for example, the first Gay Pride marches took place in US cities, including Los Angeles. They were to raise awareness of the civil rights difficulties faced by gay and lesbian people. Today, Gay Pride marches happen worldwide.

Think About This

Equality
Do you think there is real equality for everyone? Consider how physical ability, age, sex, wealth, religion, and nationality impact on people's rights. Which issues have the best equal rights and which the worst, and does this vary depending on where in the world people live?

EVENTUAL JUSTICE

Doug Jones was nine when he heard that the KKK had firebombed the 16th Street Baptist Church on 15 September 1963 and killed four girls (see page 23). The FBI suspected four men of carrying out the bombing but witnesses were reluctant to talk because they feared retaliation.

Jones studied law at university, and in 1977, witnessed the trial and conviction of one of the suspects, Robert Chambliss. But there was insufficient evidence to convict the other suspects, because some evidence was in secret FBI files. Twenty years later the FBI material was **declassified** and Jones' team reopened the case. They researched notes, photographs, and films from the 1960s and reinterviewed people to help link the suspects with the bombing. In a film they spotted one suspect, Bobby Cherry, in a mob, beating up Reverend Fred Shuttlesworth who was pastor of the church. In an FBI secret recording they heard Thomas Blanton describing how he would make a bomb. In 2001, Blanton was sent to prison for life. A year later, so was Cherry. Cases such as this illustrate how the marches were also significant because they helped create a fairer legal system.

▼ President Barack Obama and First Lady Michelle Obama walk in the inaugural parade after Obama was sworn in as the 44th President of the United States of America on 20th January 2009 in Washington, DC.

BLACK IDENTITY

The civil rights marches had a big impact on how black people viewed themselves in the Southern US states. Julia Holmes grew up in Mississippi during the years of the civil rights movement and says:

> After the movement, I think that blacks just began to feel like they were worthy, that their self-esteem just went up sky high. And they felt that they didn't have to bow down to anybody, and that they felt that they were as good.

Holmes says that the marches and other events where black and white people protested alongside each other also helped mutual understanding:

> We wouldn't be as tolerant of each other as we are now because the movement forced the races to come together and work together. Before the movement, we had all these preconceived notions about how one race was, and usually these preconceived notions were wrong.

REMEMBERING THE MARCHES

The significance of the marches has been remembered and celebrated in many different ways. For example, in Montgomery the Southern Poverty Law Center and its educational centre, the Civil Rights Memorial Center commemorate the marches but also continue the work of protesters. The centres provide legal help and advice for the poor in the South, and educate visitors about the events and significance of the civil rights movement.

Many artists have created works that help bring to life the civil rights protests. These include feature films, such as *The Long Walk Home* (1990) about the 1955 Montgomery bus boycott, and documentaries, such as *Eyes on the Prize* (1987) by Henry Hampton. This tells the story of the civil rights movement in episodes using newsreels and images. Hampton focused on the bravery and tactics of black people in the struggle because:

> A hundred civil rights stories had been told, but it was always black people being saved by whites... [the stories] depicted black folks as poor, downtrodden and brutalized primitives ... it was the strength of blacks that made the civil rights movement happen, with support from some whites.

▲ Today people in the United States mark the anniversary of Bloody Sunday each year by holding a march over the Edmund Pettus bridge outside Selma. The route is part of the Selma to Montgomery National Historic Trail that commemorates the importance of this location in the civil rights movement.

HATE CRIMES

Sadly, a small number of white extremists continued the violence towards black people even after the civil rights marches. In 1981, two KKK members lynched and killed Michael Donald in Alabama. In 2011, a 49-year-old man, James Anderson, was beaten up and then killed by a gang of white teenagers in Jackson, Mississippi. Both Donald and Anderson were chosen because they were black.

Today, racist hate crimes are investigated thoroughly by police, tried more fairly than in the past, and those found guilty are punished. For example, one KKK man was executed for his part in Donald's death, and the local Klan he belonged to was bankrupted after being ordered to pay several million dollars in damages.

SEGREGATION TODAY

In 2012, researchers analysed data about segregation in US city neighbourhoods over the previous century. They found that US cities were at their most segregated in the 1960s, but today they are more integrated than at any time since 1910. There are virtually no all-white and fewer all-black neighbourhoods than in the past. The civil rights movement reduced segregation, but people in the United States still have different expectations in life depending on their race:

- Education: test scores for children aged 9, 13, and 17 in maths and reading are consistently higher for white children, although the gap between blacks and whites has decreased since the early 1970s.
- Jobs: the unemployment rate is two times higher for black people.
- Crime: black people make up about 12 per cent of the US population but 40 per cent of the prison population, and black people generally face longer sentences than white people do.

There are many reasons for these differences, including the fact that many urban blacks live in poorer neighbourhoods where there are social problems such as ill-equipped schools with discipline problems.

▼ Young people paint murals for Martin Luther King Jr Day at a community centre in South Bronx, New York. This area of the city has high rates of poverty and crime, poor schools, and housing – all problems that King and the civil rights movement tried to change.

NEW VOTING RESTRICTIONS

Many people in the United States are also concerned about changes that could affect how many black people vote. In some states, such as Florida, only those with photo ID can vote. Poorer black people are less likely to have the time, money, or transport to obtain this new identification, so they might not vote. John Lewis, the SNCC founder and congressman, said in 2012:

> People are not being beaten and trampled by horses or tear gassed, people are not being shot and killed. The obstructions are not as obvious, but the effect ... will damage the integrity of our political process for generations to come, if it is not corrected.

HISTORY DETECTIVES: FINISHING RESEARCH?

Imagine finding a lost diary by Martin Luther King Jr detailing how he felt about the marches or other civil rights leaders. New primary sources can emerge years after an event, either accidentally or through the work of researchers. They add to what we already know and help us get closer to an accurate story of human history. So if you are starting research on a topic that has been studied and written about time and time again, remember that you might discover something new, or interpret the facts in a new way, adding to people's understanding.

> The media and history seems to record it as Martin Luther King's movement, but if young people realized that it was people just like them, their age, that formulated goals and strategies, and actually developed the movement, that when they look around now, and see things that need to be changed ... instead of saying, I wish we had a leader like Martin Luther King today, they would say, what can I do, what can my roommate and I do to effect that change.

Diane Nash

TIMELINE

1863   US President Abraham Lincoln issues the Emancipation Proclamation. This frees "all slaves in areas still in rebellion".

1865   The 13th Amendment abolishes slavery

1896   The US Supreme Court approves the "separate but equal" segregation doctrine

1909   The National Association for the Advancement of Colored People (NAACP) is formed

1925   The Ku Klux Klan marches on Washington, DC in its first national demonstration

1948   *Jul*: President Truman issues an executive order outlawing segregation in the US military

1954   *May*: The Supreme Court rules on Brown v. Board of Education, declaring that school segregation is unconstitutional

1955   *Aug*: Emmett Till is lynched
             Dec: Rosa Parks is jailed

1957   *Jan*: Martin Luther King Jr and Charles Steele establish the Southern Christian Leadership Conference (SCLC)
             Sept: The Little Rock Nine group of black students try to go to a segregated white school in Arkansas

1960   *Feb*: Four black college students begin sit-ins at a Greensboro Woolworth's
             Apr: The SNCC is formed

1961   *May*: Freedom rides are met with violence
             Nov: Albany Movement of sit-ins and protests against transport facility segregation in Albany, Georgia

1962	**Oct**: James Meredith is enrolled as the first black student at the University of Mississippi
1963	**Aug**: March on Washington for Jobs and Freedom attracts 200,000 protestors and King delivers his famous "I Have a Dream" speech **Sept**: The KKK bomb the 16th Street Baptist Church in Birmingham, Alabama, leaving four young black girls dead **Nov**: President Kennedy assassinated in Dallas; Lyndon Johnson is sworn in as the new president hours later
1964	**Jul**: Civil Rights Act makes racial discrimination illegal **Aug**: Three civil rights activists are murdered in Mississippi
1965	**Feb**: Jimmie Lee Jackson is murdered in Alabama **Mar**: A march from Selma to Montgomery, Alabama, is organized to demand protection for voting rights; segregationist state forces attack and injure protestors on Bloody Sunday; Viola Liuzzo is murdered by the KKK **Aug**: The Voting Rights Act makes it illegal to force would-be voters to pass tests in order to vote
1967	Thurgood Marshall becomes the first black Supreme Court judge
1968	**Apr**: King is assassinated in Memphis, Tennessee; President Johnson signs the Civil Rights Act of 1968 **May**: Poor People's Campaign in Washington, DC includes the last significant civil rights march, led by Coretta King
2001–2002	Bobby Cherry and Thomas Blanton are convicted for the bombing of the 16th Street Baptist Church in 1963
2005	Edgar Ray Killen is convicted of manslaughter of the three civil rights activists murdered in Mississippi in 1964
2008	Barack Obama becomes the first black US President

GLOSSARY

assassinated killed in a surprise attack

Baptist fifth largest Christian community in the world, which takes its name from the Baptist practice of immersion in water

Black Panther Party (BPP) political organization of the late 1960s that promoted increased power for black people, which could be gained by violent means

Bloody Sunday first Selma to Montgomery march, in 1965

boycott to stop using, buying, or dealing with a person, organization, or country as a protest

Brown v. Board of Education 1954 law making the segregation of schools illegal

civil rights rights of citizens to political and social freedom and equality

Civil Rights Act 1964 law banning segregation in public places and in employment on the grounds of race or religious beliefs

civil rights movement campaign in the 1950s and 1960s to change laws so that African Americans had the same rights as others

congregation group of people assembled for religious worship

declassified reduction or removal by the government of restrictions on a classified document

desegregate open a place that was previously segregated to members of all races and ethnic groups

direct action use of strikes, demonstrations, or other public forms of protest rather than negotiation to achieve one's demands

discrimination treating a particular group in society unfairly, for example because of their race or sex

emancipation freeing someone from the control of another

equality being equal in terms of status, rights, and opportunities

Federal Bureau of Investigation (FBI) US government agency that deals with both criminal investigations and information-gathering

firebombing attack with bombs designed to start fires

freedom rides bus trips taken by black and white civil rights activists in the 1960s to challenge segregation on buses

gay rights equal rights for homosexuals

gospel style of black American evangelical singing, developed from religious songs sung in Southern Baptist and Pentecostal churches

Jim Crow laws laws that kept black people from being treated as equals to whites

Ku Klux Klan (KKK) secret society that uses terrorism to promote white supremacy

lynching execution by a mob, usually by hanging

mission when people from a religious organization, especially a Christian one, travel the world to spread their faith, or the institution from which they work abroad

National Association for the Advancement of Colored People (NAACP) civil rights organization

National Guard reserve military force in the United States

persecution torment, harass, or ill-treat people, usually on the basis of their race, gender, or religion

retaliation action taken in return or in revenge for an injury or offence

segregation policy of separating people of different races, religions, or sexes and treating them in a different way

segregationist someone who believes people of different races should be kept apart

single short record with one song on each side

sit-in form of protest in which demonstrators occupy a place, refusing to leave until their demands are met

Southern Christian Leadership Conference (SCLC) civil rights organization led by religious leaders, including Martin Luther King Jr

Student Nonviolent Coordinating Committee (SNCC) civil rights organization made up mainly of young people

tear gas gas that causes severe irritation to the eyes, usually used to force crowds to disperse

the South area in the south-eastern and south-central United States

US Constitution supreme law of the United States

US Supreme Court most important court in the United States that makes decisions affecting all the states

Vietnam War war that lasted between 1954 and 1975 between the communist armies of North Vietnam supported by China and the armies of South Vietnam who were supported by the United States

voter registration requirement of citizens to register with their local board of elections before being qualified to vote

Voting Rights Act 1965 law stopping any US citizen being prevented from voting based on their race or colour and abolishing state restrictions on voter registration

White House official residence of the US president in Washington, DC

FIND OUT MORE

BOOKS

Coming of Age in Mississippi, Anne Moody (Delta, 2004)

The Civil Rights Movement (Timelines), Colin Hynson (Franklin Watts, 2010)

Warriors Don't Cry, Melba Pattillo Beals (Pocket Books, 1995)

Was the Civil Rights Movement Successful? (What Do You Think?), John
    Meany (Heinemann Library, 2008)

WEBSITES

americanhistory.si.edu/brown/history/1-segregated/jim-crow.html

Visit this website to read some of the Jim Crow laws.

www.bbc.co.uk/history/historic_figures/king_martin_luther.shtml

Learn more about Martin Luther King Jr.

www.loc.gov/teachers/classroommaterials/primarysourcesets/naacp/

This website allows you to view many primary sources from the history of
the NAACP.

memory.loc.gov/ammem/aaohtml/exhibit/aopart9.html

This website includes a summary of key moments and people in the civil
rights era, including links to primary sources.

www.pbs.org/wgbh/amex/eyesontheprize/index.html

The website of the television series *Eyes on the Prize* is a fascinating,
detailed account of the civil rights movement, including primary sources
and reflections on an era by people who were there.

photos.state.gov/libraries/iran/19452/pdfs/free-at-last.pdf

See a full summary of the civil rights movement from its beginnings with the
end of slavery to the election of President Barack Obama in 2008.

PLACES TO VISIT

There is a wide range of museums and sites focusing on civil rights in the
United States, especially in the South. If you are lucky enough to visit that
area, these are some of the places you could check out:

Birmingham Civil Rights Institute
520 Sixteenth Street North
Birmingham, Alabama 35203
www.bcri.org

Civil Rights Memorial Center
400 Washington Avenue
Montgomery, Alabama 36104
www.splcenter.org/civil-rights-memorial

Martin Luther King, Jr., Memorial
West Potomac Park
1964 Independence Avenue, SW
Washington, DC 20001
www.nps.gov/mlkm/index.htm

National Museum of African American History and Culture
1400 Constitution Avenue, NW
Washington, DC 20004
nmaahc.si.edu

TOPICS TO RESEARCH

Emancipation:
In the 19th century, some slaves in the South helped bring about emancipation by rebelling against slavery. Research the events leading up to emancipation in 1863. How do these events reflect those leading up to the Washington, DC march 100 years later?

Red Power:
In the 1960s, American Indians had the highest unemployment rates and lowest average wages of the nation, as well as suffering poor health and many negative stereotypes. Some American Indians started to fight for improved civil rights, just as African Americans were doing. Research the Declaration of Indian Purpose that led to the Red Power Movement and American Indian Movement.

INDEX